INTERMEDIATE
LOGIC

*For Christian Private
and Home Schools*

Answer Key

James B. Nance

Canon Press

MOSCOW, IDAHO

The Mars Hill Textbook Series

Introductory Logic, Doug Wilson & James B. Nance
Introductory Logic: Video Tapes featuring James B. Nance
Introductory Logic: Teacher Training Video Tapes featuring James B. Nance

Intermediate Logic, James B. Nance
Intermediate Logic: Video Tapes featuring James B. Nance
Intermediate Logic: Teacher Training Video Tapes featuring James B. Nance

Latin Primer: Book I, Martha Wilson
Latin Primer I: Video Tapes featuring Julie Garfield
Latin Primer I: Audio Pronunciation Tape featuring Julie Garfield

Latin Primer: Book II, Martha Wilson
Latin Primer II: Video Tapes featuring Julie Garfield
Latin Primer II: Audio Pronunciation Tape featuring Julie Garfield

Latin Primer: Book III, Martha Wilson
Latin Primer III: Video Tapes featuring Julie Garfield
Latin Primer III: Audio Pronunciation Tape featuring Julie Garfield

Latin Grammar: Book I, Doug Wilson & Karen Craig
Latin Grammar: Book II, Karen Craig

Matin Latin Book I, Karen Craig
Matin Latin Flashcards Book I, Karen Craig
Matin Latin Worksheet Pkt. Book I, Karen Craig
Matin Latin I: Video Tapes featuring Karen Craig

Matin Latin Book II, Karen Craig
Matin Latin Flashcards Book II, Karen Craig
Matin Latin Worksheet Pkt. Book II, Karen Craig
Matin Latin II: Video Tapes featuring Karen Craig

James B. Nance, Intrermediate Logic—Answer Key
©1996 by James B. Nance
Published by Canon Press, P.O. Box 8741, Moscow, ID 83843
800-488-2034 http://www.canonpress.org

First Edition 1996 (Rev. 2002)

Printed in the United States of America

ISBN: 1-885767-57-9

Table of Contents

DEFINITION

Exercise One

1. Define *school* with the two types of definitions identified.

    Persuasive: **An engine of propoganda.**

    Precising: **An institution for the teaching of young children**

2. Invent a new word and provide a definition for it.

    Skrink: To scratch one's head during moments of intense concentration

    What type of definition is this? **Stipulative**

3. Write an short, imaginary dialogue between two people having a verbal dispute. Then introduce a third person who settles the dispute by presenting to them lexical definitions for the word which eliminates the ambiguity.

    Smith: The commitee has concrete plans for the new School annex.

    Jones: They are not building the annex out of concrete. They are planning on using brick.

    Johnson: By 'concrete' Smith means definite, but Jones means the building material.

Exercise Two

Explain the error or problem with each genus and species hierarchy shown.

1.   ANIMALS

    MAMMALS   FISH   AIR-BREATHERS

> **MAMMALS and AIR-BREATHERS overlap (not mutuallY exclusive)**

2.   HAND

    FINGERS   THUMB   PALM

> **FINGERS, THUMB and PALM are parts of HAND, not species**

3.   TO EAT

    TO SWALLOW   TO CHEW

> **TO SWALLOW and TO CHEW are parts of TO EAT, not species.**

4.   AIRPLANE

    JET   BIPLANE   JUMBO JET

> **JUMBO JET is a species of JET (not mutually exclusive**

Fill in the genus and species hierarchy for each term given, identifying a) a genus for the term, b) another species under that genus, and c) a species of the term.

5.   a) **SPIRITUAL BEING**

    ANGEL   b) **DEMON**

    c) **ARCHANGEL**

6.   a) **FURNITURE**

    CHAIR   b) **BED**

    c) **ROCKING CHAIR**

Exercise Three

1. Arrange in order of increasing extension:
    FIGURE, PLANE FIGURE, POLYGON, RECTANGLE, SQUARE

    square, rectangle, polygon, plane figure, figure

2. Arrange in order of decreasing extension:
    INSTRUMENT, SCIMITAR, CURVED SWORD, SWORD, WEAPON

    instrument, weapon, sword, curved sword, scimitar

3. Arrange in order of increasing intension:
    ANCIENT LANGUAGE, CLASSICAL LATIN, COMMUNICATION, LANGUAGE, LATIN

    communication, language, ancient language, Latin, classical Latin

4. Arrange in order of decreasing intension:
    BAPTIST, CHRISTIAN, PROTESTANT, RELIGIOUS PERSON, SOUTHERN BAPTIST

    Southern Baptist, Baptist, Protestant, Christian, religious person

5. Draw a genus and species hierarchy which includes the following terms:
    ALGEBRA, CHEMISTRY, SUBJECT, GEOMETRY, MATH, PHYSICS, SCIENCE

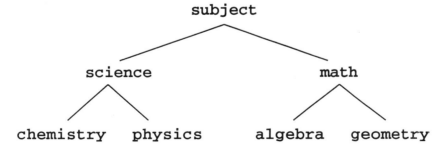

Exercise Four

Define the following terms by listing three examples of each.

1. NATION

   Japan

   Israel

   Egypt

2. BOARD GAME

   Monopoly

   Risk

   Chess

3. CANDY

   Licorice

   Lollipop

   Chocolate

Define these terms by identifying a synonym of each.

4. HAPPY

   joyous

5. JOB

   task

6. DINNER

   supper

Define the following words by genus and difference.

7. BROTHER   male sibling

8. DOE   female deer

9. WHISKER   short facial hair

10. QUEEN   female monarch

Exercise Five

> ### *A Definition Should:*
> 1. State the essential attributes of the term
> 2. Not be circular
> 3. Not be too broad or too narrow
> 4. Not be unclear or figurative
> 5. Not be negative when it can be positive
> 6. Be of the same part of speech as the term

Identify the rule(s) broken by circling the correct number(s).

RULES BROKEN

1. *Mountain:* A natural object bigger than a hill.   1   2   ③   4   5   6

2. *Wife:* Adam's rib.   ①   2   3   ④   5   6

3. *Brick:* Dried clay shaped into a brick.   1   ②   3   4   5   6

4. *Rectangle:* The shape of a typical textbook.   ①   2   3   4   5   6

5. *Headache:* When your head hurts.   1   2   ③   4   5   ⑥

6. *Capitalist:* A person who is not a socialist.   1   2   ③   4   ⑤   6

7. *To hate:* How you feel when you don't like something.   1   2   ③   4   5   ⑥

8. *Carpet:* Floor covering.   1   2   ③   4   5   6

9. *To float:* To hover.   1   ②   ③   4   5   6

10. *Bag:* A pliant repository.   1   2   3   ④   5   6

11. *Large:* Something that is not small.   1   2   3   4   ⑤   ⑥

12. *Life:* A roller coaster that we all ride.   ①   2   3   ④   5   6

Fill in the genus and species hierarchy for each term given, identifying a) a genus for the term, b) another species under that genus, and c) a species of the term.

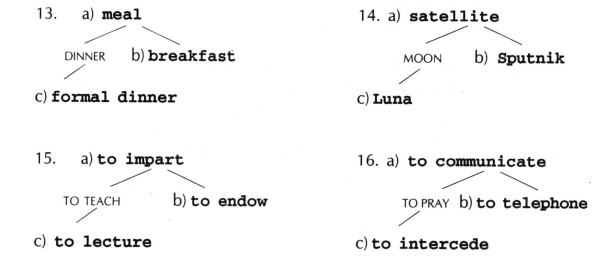

13. a) **meal**

DINNER   b) **breakfast**

c) **formal dinner**

14. a) **satellite**

MOON   b) **Sputnik**

c) **Luna**

15. a) **to impart**

TO TEACH   b) **to endow**

c) **to lecture**

16. a) **to communicate**

TO PRAY b) **to telephone**

c) **to intercede**

Define the following terms by genus and difference, using the same genus from any corresponding terms in the charts above. Be careful not to break any of the rules!

17. DINNER   **meal eaten in the evening**

18. MOON   **natural satellite**

19. WRISTWATCH   **timepiece worn on the wrist**

20. BED   **furniture used for sleeping on**

21. TO TEACH   **to impart knowledge**

22. TO PRAY   **to communicate to God**

PROPOSITIONAL LOGIC

Exercise Six

What are two main differences between propositional constants and propositional variables?

1. **abbreviated by capital letters/lower case letters**

2. **represents one given proposition/any proposition**

Use the simple proposition 'We have seen God' to create the following:

3. A truth-functional compound proposition

    We have seen God but we will not die.

4. A proposition which is *not* truth-functional

    I think we have seen God.

Circle S if the given proposition is simple. Circle C if it is compound.

5. The Lord will cause your enemies to be defeated before your eyes.
    (S) C

6. There is a way that seems right to a man but in the end it leads to death.
    S (C)

7. The fear of the Lord is the beginning of wisdom.
    (S) C

8. If we confess our sins then He is faithful to forgive us our sins.
    S (C)

9. It is false that a good tree bears bad fruit and a bad tree bears good fruit.
    S (C)

10. The Kingdom of God is not a matter of talk but of power.
    S (C)

Exercise Seven

Given: **J** means *Joseph went to Egypt.*   **F** means *There was a famine.*

              I means *Israel went to Egypt.*   **S** means *The sons of Israel became slaves.*

Translate the following symbolic propositions.

1. F • I   **There was a famine and Israel went to Egypt.**

2. ~J v S   **Joseph did not go to Egypt or the sons of Israel became slaves.**

Symbolize the following compound propositions.

3. Joseph and Israel went to Egypt.   **J • I**

4. Israel did not go to Egypt.   **~I**

5. Israel went to Egypt but his sons became slaves.   **I • S**

6. Either Joseph went to Egypt or there was a famine.   **J v F**

7. Joseph and Israel did not both go to Egypt.   **~J v ~I <u>or</u> ~(J • I)**

8. Neither Joseph nor Israel went to Egypt.   **~J • ~I <u>or</u> ~(J v I)**

9. Joseph and Israel went to Egypt; however, there was
    a famine and the sons of Israel became slaves.   **(J • I) • (F • S)**

10. Israel went to Egypt; but either Joseph did not go to
    Egypt or there was a famine.   **I • (~J v F)**

Exercise Eight

1. Fill in the following truth table to determine the truth values for the exclusive or. The truth values for p and q are filled out for you on this first one.

p	q	(p v q)	(p • q)	~(p • q)	(p v q) • ~(p • q)
T	T	T	T	F	F
T	F	T	F	T	T
F	T	T	F	T	T
F	F	F	F	T	F

2. Determine the truth values for ~(J • R) and ~J • ~R to prove that they are different. The initial J and R should follow the same pattern as p and q in problem one.

J	R	~J	~R	(J • R)	~(J • R)	~J • ~R
T	T	F	F	T	F	F
T	F	F	T	F	T	F
F	T	T	F	F	T	F
F	F	T	T	F	T	T

3. Write sentences in English corresponding to the two compound propositions in problem two, using *Joe is a student* for J and *Rachel is a student* for R.

~(J • R)   Joe and Rachel are not both students.

~J • ~R   Both Joe and Rachel are not students.

Determine the truth value for each compound proposition. Assume that propositions A and B are true, X and Y are false. Circle T if the entire compound proposition is true. Circle F if it is false. Use the space at the right for showing any work.

4.   ~A ∨ B   Ⓣ   F

A	B	~A	~A∨B
T	T	F	T

5.   X ∨ ~B   T   Ⓕ

X	B	~B	X∨~B
F	T	F	F

6.   ~(A ∨ B)   T   Ⓕ

A	B	A∨B	~(A∨B)
T	T	T	F

7.   (A • X) ∨ (B • Y)   T   Ⓕ

A	X	B	Y	A•X	B•Y	(A•X)∨(B•Y)
T	F	T	F	F	F	F

8.   ~[X ∨ (Y • ~A)]   Ⓣ   F

X	Y	A	~A	Y•~A	X∨(Y•~A)	~[X∨(Y•~A)]
F	F	T	F	F	F	T

Identify the truth value of each of the following sentences by circling T or F.

9.   Jonah was a prophet or Isaiah was a prophet.
     Ⓣ   F

10. Jeremiah was not a prophet but Isaiah was a prophet.
     T   Ⓕ

11. It is not true that both Jeremiah was a prophet and Isaiah was not a prophet.
     Ⓣ   F

12. Jonah was not a prophet or both Jeremiah and Isaiah were not prophets.
     T   Ⓕ

13. A false proposition is not true.
     Ⓣ   F

14. It is false that a true proposition is not false.
     T   Ⓕ

15. It is true that it is false that a true proposition is not false.
     T   Ⓕ

Exercise Nine

1.   Develop the truth table for the compound proposition ~p v q on the line below.

p	q	~p	~p v q
T	T	F	T
T	F	F	F
F	T	T	T
F	F	T	T

2.   To what compound proposition is ~p v q equivalent?   **p ⊃ q**

If A, B and C represent true propositions and X, Y and Z represent false propositions, determine whether the following compound propositions are true or false and circle the appropriate letter.

3.   A ⊃ B   (T)   F

4.   B ⊃ Z   T   (F)

5.   X ⊃ C   (T)   F

6.   (A ⊃ B) ⊃ Z   T   (F)

7.   X ⊃ (Y ⊃ Z)   (T)   F

8.   (A ⊃ Y) v (B ⊃ ~C)   T   (F)

9.   [(X ⊃ Z) ⊃ C] ⊃ Z   T   (F)

10. [(A • X) ⊃ Y] ⊃ [(X ⊃ ~Z) v (A ⊃ Y)]   (T)   F

If S represents *I will go swimming* and C represents *The water is cold*, symbolize the following:

11. If the water is not cold then I will go swimming.   ~C ⊃ S

12. I will go swimming if the water is cold.   C ⊃ S

Exercise Ten

Set up the biconditional for each pair of propositions to determine if they are logically equivalent, contradictory, or neither. In this exercise, do not use guide columns. Rather, place the truth values immediately beneath the variables and work outward. Problem 4 will require eight rows.

1. [~(p v q)] ≡ (~p v ~q)

```
F TTT   T   FTFFT
F TTF   F   FTTTF
F FTT   F   TFTFT
T FFF   T   TFTTF
```

        neither

2. (p ⊃ q) ≡ (~q ⊃ ~p)

```
TTT   T   FTTFT
TFF   T   TFFFT
FTT   T   FTTTF
FTF   T   TFTTF
```

        equivalent

3. [~(~p v q)] ≡ (p ⊃ q)

```
F FTTT   F   TTT
T FTFF   F   TFF
F TFTT   F   FTT
F TFTF   F   FTF
```

     contradictory

4. [p ⊃ (q ⊃ r)] ≡ [(p ⊃ q) ⊃ r]

```
TT TTT   T   TTT TT
TF TFF   T   TTT FF
TT FTT   T   TFF TT
TT FTF   T   TFF TF
FT TTT   T   FTT TT
FT TFF   F   FTT FF
FT FTT   T   FTF TT
FT FTF   F   FTF FF
```

        neither

5. Write a set of propositions in English which could be symbolized by problem #2.

If a platypus is a mammal then it is warm-blooded.

If a platypus is not warm-blooded then it is not a mammal.

Determine the truth value for each compound proposition. Assume that propositions A and B are true, X and Y are false, and P and Q are unknown. Circle **T** if the proposition is true, circle **F** if it is false, circle **?** if the truth value cannot be determined. (Hint: There are two of each.)

		T	F	?
1.	P v ~P	(T)	F	?
2.	(P ⊃ P) ⊃ ~A	T	(F)	?
3.	(Y ⊃ P) ⊃ Q	T	F	(?)
4.	P ⊃ (X v Y)	T	F	(?)
5.	~Q • [(P v Q) • ~P]	T	(F)	?
6.	~[P v (B • Y)] v [(P v B) • (P v Y)]	(T)	F	?

Use truth tables to determine the validity of the following arguments.

7.	p v q	~p	∴ q		8.	p ⊃ q	∴ p ⊃ (p • q)
	T	F	T			T	T ←VALID
	T	F	F			F	F
	T	T	T ←VALID			T	T ←VALID
	F	T	F			T	T ←VALID

9.	p • q	∴ p v q		10.	p ⊃ ~q	~q	∴ p
	T	T ←VALID			F	F	T
	F	T			T	T	T
	F	T			T	F	F
	F	F			T	T	F ←INVALID

11. If Jesus was John the Baptist raised from the dead, then He could do miracles. Jesus did miracles, so He was John the Baptist raised from the dead. (**J** means *Jesus was John the Baptist raised from the dead,* **M** means *He could do miracles.*)

J ⊃ M	M	∴ J
T	T	T
F	F	T
T	T	F ←INVALID
T	F	F

12. If Jeff studies then he will get good grades. If Jeff does not study then he will play. So Jeff will either get good grades or he will play. (**S** means *Jeff studies,* **G** means *He will get good grades,* **P** means *He will play.*)

S ⊃ G	~S ⊃ P	∴ G v P	
T	T	T	←Valid
T	T	T	←Valid
F	T	T	
F	T	F	
T	T	T	←Valid
T	F	T	
T	T	T	←Valid
T	F	F	

13. If Jesus is not God then He was a liar or He was insane. Jesus was clearly not a liar. He certainly was not insane. We conclude that Jesus is God. (**G** means *Jesus is God,* **L** means *He was a liar,* **I** means *He was insane.*)

~G ⊃ (L v I)	~L	~I	∴ G	
T	F	F	T	
T	F	T	T	
T	T	F	T	
T	T	T	T	←Valid
T	F	F	F	
T	F	T	F	
T	T	F	F	
F	T	T	F	

14. If taxes increase then the public will complain, but if the deficit increases then the public will complain. Either taxes or the deficit will increase. Thus the public is bound to complain. (**T** means *Taxes increase,* **P** means *The public will complain,* **D** means *The deficit increases.*)

T ⊃ P	D ⊃ P	T v D	∴ P	
T	T	T	T	←Valid
T	T	T	T	←Valid
F	F	T	F	
F	T	T	F	
T	T	T	T	←Valid
T	T	F	T	
T	F	T	F	
T	T	F	F	

Exercise Twelve

On a *separate sheet of paper,* use truth tables to determine the validity of the propositional arguments below. (Problems four and five require eight rows each, problem six requires sixteen!)

1.

p	∴ ~p ∨ q
T	**T**
T	**F** ←Invalid
F	**T**
F	**T**

2.

p ⊃ q	∴ ~q ⊃ ~p
T	**T** ←Valid
F	**F**
T	**T** ←Valid
T	**T** ←Valid

3.

p ⊃ q	~q	∴ p ≡ q
T	**F**	**T**
F	**T**	**F**
T	**F**	**F**
T	**T**	**T** ←Valid

4.

p ⊃ (q ⊃ r)	q	∴ r ⊃ p
T	**T**	**T**
F	**T**	**T**
T	**F**	**T**
T	**F**	**T**
T	**T**	**F** ←Invalid
T	**T**	**T**
T	**F**	**F**
T	**F**	**T**

p ⊃ (~q ⊃ r)	p	∴ ~r ⊃ q	
T	T	T	←Vᴀʟɪᴅ
T	T	T	←Vᴀʟɪᴅ
T	T	T	←Vᴀʟɪᴅ
F	T	F	
T	F	T	
T	F	T	
T	F	T	
T	F	F	

(p ⊃ q) • [(p • q) ⊃ r]	p ⊃ (r ⊃ s)	∴ p ⊃ s	
T	T	T	←Vᴀʟɪᴅ
T	F	F	
F	T	T	
F	T	F	
F	T	T	
F	F	F	
F	T	T	
F	T	F	
T	T	T	
T	T	T	
T	T	T	
T	T	T	
T	T	T	
T	T	T	
T	T	T	
T	T	T	

} Vᴀʟɪᴅ

Exercise Thirteen

Determine the validity of the following arguments using the shorter truth-table method. Use the constants given in order of appearance in the argument to symbolize each proposition.

1. If I study for my test tonight then I am sure to pass it, but if I watch TV then I will get to see my favorite show. So if I study for the test and watch TV, then I will either pass the test or I will see my favorite show. (S, P, W, F)

S ⊃ P	W ⊃ F	∴ (S • W) ⊃ (P v F)
T T F	T T F	T T T F F F F
↖	↖	VALID

2. If Caesar had been a benevolent king, then all Romans would have received their full rights under the law. The Roman Christians were persecuted for their faith. If all Romans had received their full rights, then the Roman Christians would not have been persecuted. Therefore Caesar was not a benevolent king. (B, R, P)

B ⊃ R	P	R ⊃ ~P	∴ ~B
T T F	T	F T FT	FT
↖			VALID

3. If I promise to feed the dog and bathe it, and if I promise to clean up after the dog's messes, then my mother will let me keep it. If promising to clean up after the dog's messes implies that mother will let me keep the dog, then if I pay for the dog with my own money then I will be allowed to name it myself. I will pay for the dog with my own money. Therefore, if I promise to feed the dog then I will be allowed to name it myself. (F, B, C, K, P, N)

[(F • B) • C] ⊃ K	(C ⊃ K) ⊃ (P ⊃ N)	P	∴ F ⊃ N
T F F F T T F	T F F T T F F	T	T F F
			INVALID

4.   If the book of Hebrews is Scripture then it was written by Paul or Apollos. If Paul wrote anonymously to the Hebrews then he wrote anonymously in some of his letters. If Hebrews was written by Paul then he wrote anonymously to the Hebrews. Paul did not write anonymously in any of his letters. The book of Hebrews is Scripture. Therefore Hebrews was written by Apollos. (S, P, A, H, L)

S	⊃	(P	v	A)		H	⊃	L		P	⊃	H		~L		S		∴	A
T	T	F	F	F		F	T	F		F	T	F		T F		T			F

VALID

5.   If you sin apart from the law then you will perish apart from the law, but if you sin under the law then you will be judged by the law. If you sin, then you either sin apart from the law or you sin under the law. You do sin. Therefore you will either perish apart from the law or you will be judged by the law. (A, P, U, J, S)

A	⊃	P		U	⊃	J		S	⊃	(A	v	U)		S		∴	P	v	J
F	T	F		F	T	F		T	T	F	T	F		T			F	F	F

VALID

6.   If you obey the law then you will not be condemned. You have not obeyed the law. You will be condemned. (O, C)

O	⊃	~C		~O		∴	C
F	T	T F		T F			F

INVALID

7-12. Determine the validity of the arguments in exercise twelve using the shorter truth-table method.

7.   p   ∴ ~p v q
   ——————   ————————
    T   F T F F

                              INVALID

8.   p ⊃ q   ∴ ~q ⊃ ~p
   ——————————   ——————————————
   T T F   T F F F T
      ↖

                              VALID

9.   p ⊃ q   ~q   ∴ p ≡ q
   ——————————   ————   ——————————
   T T F   T F   T F F
      ↖

                              VALID

10.   p ⊃ (q ⊃ r)   q   ∴ r ⊃ p
   ——————————————   ———   ————————
   F T T T T   T   T F F

                              INVALID

11.   p ⊃ (~q ⊃ r)   p   ∴ ~r ⊃ q
   ——————————————   ———   ——————————
   T T T F F F   T   T F F F
         ↖

                              VALID

12.   (p ⊃ q) • [(p • q) ⊃ r]   p ⊃ (r ⊃ s)   ∴ p ⊃ s
   ————————————————————————————   ——————————————   ————————
   T T T T T T T T F   T T F T F   T F F
                  ↖

                              VALID

Exercise Fourteen

Use the shorter truth-table method to determine the validity of the following arguments. Most of these (but not all) will require you to guess a truth value.

1.   p ≡ q   q ≡ r   ∴ p ≡ r
     T T F   F T F   T F F
        ↖
                                            VALID
     F T T   T T T   F F T
        ↖

2.   p v q   ∴ p • q
     T T F   T F F   INVALID

3.   p ⊃ q   q ≡ r   ∴ p ⊃ r
     T T F   F T F   T F F
        ↖
                                            VALID

4.   (p ⊃ q) v (r ⊃ s)   p v r   ∴ q v s
      T F F T F T F   T T F   F F F   INVALID

5.   p v q   ~ [q • (r ⊃ p)]   ∴ ~ (p ≡ q)
     T T T   T T F   T T   F T T T
                          ↖
     F T F   T F F   F   F F T F   VALID
        ↖

6.   p ⊃ (q ⊃ r)   q ⊃ (p ⊃ r)   ∴ (p v q) ⊃ r
     T T F T F   F T T F F   T T F F F   INVALID

Exercise Fifteen

Using the shorter truth-table method, determine the consistency, of the following proposition sets. With problems 6 and 7, use the constants given.

1.

p	~p ⊃ r
T	F T T

consistent

2.

~ ~p	~p • q
T F T	F T T
	↖

inconsistent

3.

p ⊃ q	p	~q
T T F	T	T F
↖		

inconsistent

4.

p v q	~p
F T T	T F

consistent

5.

p ≡ q	q ≡ r	p	~r
T T F	F T F	T	T F
↖			

inconsistent

6.   Mr. Copia owns a Porsche and a mansion. *If he doesn't own a mansion then he either owns a Porsche or it's my imagination.* It's your imagination. (P, M, I)

P • M	~M ⊃ (P v I)	I	
T T T	F T T T T T	T	consistent

7.   If I learn grammar or logic then I can use rhetoric. *If you can't use rhetoric then you learn grammar and logic.* (G, L, R)

(G v L) ⊃ R	~R ⊃ (G • L)	
T T	F T T	consistent

Exercise Sixteen

Using the shorter truth-table method, determine the equivalence of each pair of propositions.

1.
$$\underline{\sim (p \bullet q) \qquad \sim p \vee \sim q}$$
T T F T   FT F FT
                    ↖
F T T T   FT T FT
                         ↖

EQUIVALENT

2.
$$\underline{p \supset q \qquad p \supset (p \bullet q)}$$
T T F   TF TFF
    ↖
T F F   TT TFF
                    ↖

EQUIVALENT

3.
$$\underline{p \vee (p \supset q) \qquad q \supset p}$$
FT FT T   T F F

NOT EQUIVALENT

4.
$$\underline{p \qquad p \vee (p \bullet q)}$$
T   T F
               ↖
F   FT FF
               ↖

EQUIVALENT

5. If Christ's righteousness is not imputed to you then you are condemned.
   Either Christ's righteousness is imputed to you or you are condemned.

$$\underline{\sim I \supset C \qquad\qquad I \vee C}$$
TF T F   F F F
     ↖
TF F F   F T F   **EQUIVALENT**
                       ↖

CHALLENGE: Is $\underline{[(\sim p \bullet r) \vee (q \bullet r)]}$ equivalent to $\underline{[(p \supset q) \bullet r]}$?   **Yes**
FT FT F FFT   TTF TT
                          ↖
FT FT T FFT   TFF FT
         ↖
FF T FF   FF
    ↖

Exercise Seventeen

Symbolize the dilemma from the middle of the previous page. Then symbolize the counter-dilemma below it. Use shorter truth tables to demonstrate the validity of both arguments.

1. The dilemma: (S ⊃ M) • (~S ⊃ F)   S v ~S   ∴ M v F

                            F T F   T   TF T F   F T TF   F F F

2. The counter-dilemma:

    (S ⊃ ~F) • (~S ⊃ ~M)   S v ~S   ∴ ~F v ~M

     T T FT   T   FT T FT   T   FT F FT

       ↖

Explain how you could deal with each of the following dilemmas, stating which of the three methods you use:

3. If angels are material, then they cannot all simultaneously fit on the head of a pin. If angels are immaterial, then they can neither dance nor be in contact with the top of a pin. Angels are either material or immaterial. Either way, all the angels that exist cannot simultaneously dance on the head of a pin.

    You can <u>grasp a horn</u> by denying the first conditional as follows: "Even if angels are material, they could fit on the head of a pin by being very small."

4. If you sin apart from the law then you will perish apart from the law, but if you sin under the law then you will be judged by the law. You either sin apart from the law or you sin under the law. Therefore you will either perish apart from the law or you will be judged by the law.

    You could <u>grasp it by the horns</u> by denying both conditionals as follows: "If I sin I will not necessarily perish, not if I have been justfied by faith."

5. If Congressman Jones lied about the sale of arms then he should not be re-elected. Neither should he be re-elected if he honestly couldn't remember something so important. He either lied or he couldn't remember, so he should not be re-elected.

You could <u>go between the horns</u>, saying "He didn't lie, and he did remember, but he chose to conceal the truth for the good of the people."

6. If taxes increase then the public will complain, but if the deficit increases then the public will complain. Either taxes or the deficit will increase. Thus the public is bound to complain.

You could <u>rebut it</u> with this counter-dilemma: "If taxes increase then the deficit will go down. If taxes decrease then the public won't complain. Either taxes increase or they decrease; either way the public won't complain."

7. Modern prophets either prophesy falsely or truly. If they prophesy falsely, they should be rejected, but if truly, their prophecies must be accepted as equal to Scripture. So their words should either be rejected or accepted as equal to Scripture.

You could <u>grasp a horn</u> by denying the second conditional as follows: "Even if they prophesy truly, their prophecies do not speak of the same truths as Scripture and should not be accepted as equal to it."

8. If God were perfectly good then He would be willing to prevent evil, and if God were infinitely powerful then He would be able to prevent evil. But God is either unwilling or unable to prevent evil. Therefore He is either not perfectly good or He is not infinitely powerful.

You could <u>grasp a horn</u> by denying the first conditional: "God is perfectly good, but he allows evil to continue for a greater purpose of bringing good out of it, such as at the crucifixion."

FORMAL PROOFS OF VALIDITY

Exercise Eighteen

Verify the validity of the rules of inference using the shorter truth-table method.

1. *Modus Ponens* (M.P.)

$$p \supset q \qquad p \qquad \therefore q$$

T T F	T	F
↖		

2. *Modus Tollens* (M.T.)

$$p \supset q \qquad \sim q \qquad \therefore \sim p$$

T T F	T F	F T
↖		

3. *Hypothetical Syllogism* (H.S.)

$$p \supset q \qquad q \supset r \qquad \therefore p \supset r$$

T T F	F T F	T F F
↖		

4. *Disjunctive Syllogism* (D.S.)

$$p \lor q \qquad \sim p \qquad \therefore q$$

F T F	T F	F
↖		

5. *Constructive Dilemma* (C.D.)

$$(p \supset q) \bullet (r \supset s) \qquad p \lor r \qquad \therefore q \lor s$$

F T F T F T F	F T F	F F F
↖		

6. *Absorption* (Abs.)

$$p \supset q \qquad \therefore p \supset (p \bullet q)$$

T T F	T F T F F
↖	

7. *Simplification* (Simp.)

$$p \bullet q \qquad \therefore p$$

F T	F
↖	

8. *Addition* (Add.)

$$p \qquad \therefore p \lor q$$

T	T F
	↖

9. *Conjunction* (Conj.)

$$p \qquad q \qquad \therefore p \bullet q$$

T	T	T F T
		↖

Exercise Nineteen

Identify the rule of inference used in each of the following arguments. You may abbreviate.

1. A v B
    ~A
    ∴ B   **D.S.**

2. X
    X ⊃ Y
    ∴ X • (X ⊃ Y)   **Conj.**

3. (Q ⊃ R) • (~Q ⊃ T)
    Q v ~Q
    ∴ R v T   **C.D.**

4. (C ⊃ D) ⊃ E
    C ⊃ D
    ∴ E   **M.P.**

5. ~U ⊃ (V v X)
    (V v X) ⊃ W
    ∴ ~U ⊃ W   **H.S.**

6. (F • ~G) ⊃ ~H
    ~ ~H
    ∴ ~(F • ~G)   **M.T.**

7. (A ⊃ B) • (C ⊃ D)
    ∴ A ⊃ B   **Simp.**

8. S v T
    ∴ (S v T) v R   **Add.**

9. J ⊃ ~K
    ∴ J ⊃ (J • ~K)   **Abs.**

For the following formal proofs of validity, give the justification for each step.

10. 1. A v B
    2. A ⊃ C
    3. ~C / ∴ B
    4. ~A   2,3 M.T.
    5. B   1,4 D.S.

11. 1. P ⊃ Q
    2. R
    3. P / ∴ R • Q
    4. Q   1,3 M.P.
    5. R • Q   2,4 Conj.

12. 1. ~M ⊃ N
    2. L ⊃ ~M
    3. L / ∴ L • N
    4. L ⊃ N   2,1 H.S.
    5. L ⊃ (L • N) 4 Abs.
    6. L • N   5,3 M.P.

13. 1. X ⊃ Y
    2. X
    3. W ⊃ Z / ∴ Y v Z
    4. (X ⊃ Y) • (W ⊃ Z) 1,3 Conj.
    5. X v W   2 Add.
    6. Y v Z   4,5 C.D.

14. 1. ~F • G
    2. H ⊃ F / ∴ ~H v G
    3. ~F   1 Simp.
    4. ~H   2,3 M.T.
    5. ~H v G   4 Add.

15. 1. A
    2. ~A / ∴ B
    3. A v B   1 Add.
    4. B   3,2 D.S.

16. 1.   D ⊃ E
     2.   (D • E) ⊃ (F • G)
     3.   D   / ∴ F
     4.   D ⊃ (D • E)   **1 Abs.**
     5.   D ⊃ (F • G)   **4,2 H.S.**
     6.   F • G   **5,3 M.P.**
     7.   F   **6 Simp.**

CHALLENGE: Re-write the proof in problem 13 in one less step.

1. X ⊃ Y
2. X
3. W ⊃ Z / ∴ Y v Z
4. Y   1,2 M.P.
5. Y v Z   4 Add.

Exercise Twenty

Determine which rule of inference is used in each of the following arguments.

1. If I sin then I will be disciplined for sinning. Therefore if I
    sin then I will both sin and be disciplined for sinning.   **Abs.**

2. Jesus is Man. Jesus is God. So Jesus is both Man and God.   **Conj.**

3. If Jesus is living then He is my Savior, but if Jesus did not
    rise from the dead then my faith is futile. Either Jesus is living
    or He did not rise from the dead. Thus either Jesus is my
    Savior or my faith is futile.   **C.D.**

4. If God gave the law then it should be obeyed. God gave the
    law. We conclude that it should be obeyed.   **M.P.**

5. Jesus was either a bad man or He was God. Jesus was not a
    bad man. Therefore He must have been God.   **D.S.**

6. Ezekiel and Jeremiah were both prophets. Thus Ezekiel was
    a prophet.   **Simp.**

7. If Ruth was a Gentile then Boaz married a Gentile. If Boaz
    married a Gentile then King David was part Gentile. So if
    Ruth was a Gentile then King David was part Gentile.   **H.S.**

8. Judas betrayed Christ. So Judas betrayed Christ or he
    killed himself.   **Add.**

9. If you loved God then you would love your neighbor. You
    do not love your neighbor. It is obvious that you do not
    love God.   **M.T.**

Use the shorter truth-table method to determine the validity of the following arguments.

10. If God desires every man to be saved then if God's desires are always ful-filled then every man will be saved. Every man will not be saved. Therefore it is false that both God desires every man to be saved and that God's desires are always fulfilled. (D, F, E)

```
D ⊃ (F ⊃ E)        ~E            ∴ ~(D • F)
T T   T F F              TF              F T T T
      ↖                                          VALID
```

11. If Mary Magdalene was with the women in the tomb then she would have seen a vision of angels. If she saw a vision of angels then she would have told the apostles about a vision of angels. She told the apostles about a vision of angels. Therefore Mary Magdalene saw a vision of angels and she was with the women in the tomb. (W, V, T)

```
W ⊃ V        V ⊃ T          T            ∴ V • W
F T T        T T T          T              T F F
                                                    INVALID
```

12. If the first-century Christians were taught that Jesus was coming soon, and if the word "coming" means His final coming, and if "soon" means within a cen-tury, then the final coming occurred before the end of the second century. The final coming did not occur before the end of the second century. The first century Christians were taught that Jesus was coming soon. Therefore, either the word "coming" does not mean His final coming, or the word "soon" does not mean within a century. (F, C, S, B)

```
[(F • C) • S] ⊃ B        ~B            F            ∴ ~C v ~S
  T T T   T T   T F        TF            T              FT F FT
              ↖                                                  VALID
```

Exercise Twenty-one

Provide the justification for each step in the following formal proofs of validity.

1.
  1. P v Q
  2. ~P
  3. Q ⊃ R   /∴ R
  4. Q   **1,2 D.S.**
  5. R   **3,4 M.P.**

2.
  1. X ⊃ Y
  2. W ⊃ Z
  3. X v W   /∴ Y v Z
  4. (X ⊃ Y) • (W ⊃ Z)   **1,2 Conj.**
  5. Y v Z   **4,3 C.D.**

3.
  1. ~A • B
  2. C ⊃ A
  3. C v D   /∴ D
  4. ~A   **1 Simp.**
  5. ~C   **2,4 M.T.**
  6. D   **3,5 D.S.**

4.
  1. F ⊃ G
  2. H ⊃ F
  3. ~(H • G)   /∴ ~H
  4. H ⊃ G   **2,1 H.S.**
  5. H ⊃ (H • G)   **4 Abs.**
  6. ~H   **5,3 M.T.**

5.
  1. M • L
  2. (M v N) ⊃ P   /∴ P
  3. M   **1 Simp.**
  4. M v N   **3 Add.**
  5. P   **2,4 M.P.**

6.
  1. P ⊃ Q
  2. S
  3. Q ⊃ R   /∴ (P ⊃ R) • S
  4. P ⊃ R   **1,3 H.S.**
  5. (P ⊃ R) • S   **4,2 Conj.**

Construct a formal proof for each of the following arguments in the number of steps given.

7.
  1. A • B   /∴ A v B
  2. **A**   **1 Simp.**
  3. **A v B**   **2 Add.**

8.
  1. C ⊃ D
  2. (C • D) ⊃ E   /∴ C ⊃ E
  3. **C ⊃ (C • D)**   **1 Abs.**
  4. **C ⊃ E**   **3,2 H.S.**

9.
  1. F v G
  2. ~F   /∴ G • ~F
  3. **G**   **1,2 D.S.**
  4. **G • ~F**   **3,2 Conj.**

10.
  1. (H ⊃ I) • (J ⊃ K)
  2. H   /∴ I v K
  3. **H v J**   **2 Add.**
  4. **I v K**   **1,3 C.D.**

11. 1. M • L
    2. (M v N) ⊃ O / ∴ O
    3. M   1 Simp.
    4. M v N   3 Add.
    5. O   2,4 M.P.

12. 1. P ⊃ Q
    2. Q ⊃ R
    3. ~R / ∴ ~P
    4. P ⊃ R   1,2 H.S.
    5. ~P   4,3 M.T.

13. 1. S ⊃ T
    2. S v U
    3. ~T / ∴ U • ~S
    4. ~S   1,3 M.T.
    5. U   2,4 D.S.
    6. U • ~S   5,4 Conj.

14. 1. V ⊃ W
    2. X ⊃ V
    3. ~(X • W) / ∴ ~X
    4. X ⊃ W   2,1 H.S.
    5. X ⊃ (X • W)   4 Abs.
    6. ~X   5,3 M.T.

15. 1. Y ⊃ Z
    2. (Y • Z) ⊃ A
    3. ~(Y • A) / ∴ ~Y
    4. Y ⊃ (Y • Z) 1 Abs.
    5. Y ⊃ A   4,2 H.S.
    6. Y ⊃ (Y • A) 5 Abs.
    7. ~Y   6,3 M.T.

16. 1. B ⊃ C
    2. D ⊃ E
    3. D v B
    4. ~E / ∴ C
    5. ~D   2,4 M.T.
    6. B   3,5 D.S.
    7. C   1,6 M.P.

Exercise Twenty-two

"The sons of God were either righteous men or they were angels. If they were righteous then they would have pleased God. They did not please God. Thus they must have been angels." (See Genesis 6:1-5) (R, A, P)

1. Prove the validity of the above argument using the shorter truth-table method.

R v A	R ⊃ P	~P	∴ A
F T F	F T F	T F	F

VALID

2. Write the formal proof of validity.

```
1. R v A
2. R   P
3. ~P  / ∴ A
4. ~R          2,3 M. T.
5. A           1,4 D. S.
        QED
```

3. Re-write the argument and its proof in ordinary English as a dialogue between two people. Imagine that one is trying to convince the other of the truth of the conclusion by stepping him through the formal proof (without mentioning the justification for each step).

> "We can prove that the sons of God were angels."
> "How?"
> "Well, if the sons of God were righteous men then they would have pleased God. But we know they didn't please God. So they were not righteous men."
> "Yeah, so?"
> "The only two options seem to be that they were either righteous men or angels. We have seen that they were not righteous men. We must conclude that they were angels."
> "I see."

Exercise Twenty-three

Identify the rule of replacement used. Use the abbreviations.

1. A ≡ (A v A)
    Taut.

2. (M • N) ≡ ~ ~(M • N)
    D.N.

3. [(R ⊃ S) ⊃ T] ≡ [~(R ⊃ S) v T]
    Impl.

4. (X • Y) ≡ (Y • X)
    Com.

5. ~(P • Q) ≡ (~P v ~Q)
    DeM.

6. (F ⊃ G) ≡ (~G ⊃ ~F)
    Trans.

7. [(B v C) v D] ≡ [B v (C v D)]
    Assoc.

8. [J ⊃ (K ⊃ L)] ≡ [(J • K) ⊃ L]
    Exp.

9. [X v (Y • Z)] ≡ [(X v Y) • (X v Z)]
    Dist.

10. (W ≡ V) ≡ [(W ⊃ V) • (V ⊃ W)]
    Equiv.

Justify each step for the following proofs of validity.

11. 1. P ⊃ Q
    2. R ⊃ ~Q / ∴ P ⊃ ~R
    3. ~ ~Q ⊃ ~R   **2 Trans.**
    4. Q ⊃ ~R   **3 D.N.**
    5. P ⊃ ~R   **1,4 H.S.**

12. 1. (P • Q) ⊃ R
    2. (P ⊃ R) ⊃ S   / ∴ Q ⊃ S
    3. (Q • P) ⊃ R   **1 Com.**
    4. Q ⊃ (P ⊃ R)   **3 Exp.**
    5. Q ⊃ S   **4,2 H.S.**

13. 1. (P • Q) ⊃ R
    2. ~R   / ∴ P ⊃ ~Q
    3. ~(P • Q)   **1,2 M.T.**
    4. ~P v ~Q   **3 DeM.**
    5. P ⊃ ~Q   **4 Impl.**

14. 1. P ⊃ ~Q / ∴ ~Q v (Q • ~P)
    2. ~ ~Q ⊃ ~P   **1 Trans.**
    3. Q ⊃ ~P   **2 D.N.**
    4. Q ⊃ (Q • ~P)   **3 Abs.**
    5. ~Q v (Q • ~P)   **4 Impl.**

15. 1. (P v Q) ⊃ (R • S)
    2. ~R   / ∴ ~P
    3. ~R v ~S   **2 Add.**
    4. ~(R • S)   **3 DeM.**
    5. ~(P v Q)   **1,4 M.T.**
    6. ~P • ~Q   **5 DeM.**
    7. ~P   **6 Simp.**

16. 1. (P v Q) ⊃ [R • (S • T)]
    2. Q   / ∴ R • S
    3. Q v P   **2 Add.**
    4. P v Q   **3 Com.**
    5. R • (S • T)   **1,4 M.P.**
    6. (R • S) • T   **5 Assoc.**
    7. R • S   **6 Simp.**

17. 1.   (P v ~Q) v R
     2.   ~P v (Q • ~P)   / ∴ Q ⊃ R
     3.   (~P v Q) • (~P v ~P)   **2 Dist.**
     4.   (~P v ~P) • (~P v Q)   **3 Com.**
     5.   ~P v ~P   **4 Simp.**
     6.   ~P   **5 Taut.**
     7.   P v (~Q v R)   **1 Assoc.**
     8.   ~Q v R   **7,6 D.S.**
     9.   Q ⊃ R   **8 Impl.**

18. 1.   P • (Q v R)
     2.   P ⊃ [Q ⊃ (S • T)]
     3.   (P • R) ⊃ ~(S v T)   / ∴ S ≡ T
     4.   (P • Q) ⊃ (S • T)   **2 Exp.**
     5.   (P • R) ⊃ (~S • ~T)   **3 DeM.**
     6.   [(P • Q) ⊃ (S • T)] • [(P • R) ⊃ (~S • ~T)]   **4,5 Conj.**
     7.   (P • Q) v (P • R)   **1 Dist.**
     8.   (S • T) v (~S • ~T)   **6,7 C.D.**
     9.   S ≡ T   **8 Equiv.**

Exercise Twenty-four

Write a formal proof of validity for each of the following arguments.

1. 1. A /∴ B ⊃ A   2. 2. C ⊃ (D ⊃ E) /∴ D ⊃ (C ⊃ E)
    2. **A v ~B   1 Add.**   2. **(C • D) ⊃ E   1 Exp.**
    3. **~B v A   2 Com.**   3. **(D • C) ⊃ E   2 Com.**
    4. **B ⊃ A   3 Impl.**   4. **D ⊃ (C E)   3 Exp.**

3. 1. F ⊃ (G • H) /∴ F ⊃ G   4. 1. I ⊃ J /∴ I ⊃ (J v K)
    2. **~F v (G • H) 1 Impl.**   2. **~I v J   1 Impl.**
    3. **(~F v G) • (~F v H) 3.**   **(~I v J) v K 2 Add.**
                   2 Dist.   4. **~I v (J vK)   3 Assoc.**
    4. **~F v G   3 Simp.**   5. **I ⊃ (J • K)   4 Impl.**
    5. **F ⊃ G   4 Impl.**

5. 1. L ⊃ N /∴ (L • M) ⊃ N   6. 1. P ⊃ Q
    2. **(L N) v ~M 1 Add.**   2. ~Q /∴ P ≡ Q
    3. **~M v (L ⊃ N) 2 Com.**   3. **~Q v P   2 Add.**
    4. **M ⊃ (L ⊃ N) 3 Impl.**   4. **Q ⊃ P   3 Impl.**
    5. **(M • L) ⊃ N   4 Exp.**   5. **(P ⊃ Q) • (Q ⊃ P)**
    6. **(L • M) ⊃ N   5 Com.**   **1,4 Conj.**
                                        6. **P ≡ Q   5 Equiv.**

7. 1. ~R ⊃ (S v T)   8. 1. U ⊃ W
    2. ~S   2. ~(U ⊃ X) /∴ W
    3. ~T /∴ R   3. **~(~U v X)   2 Impl.**
    4. **~S • ~T   2,3 Conj.**   4. **~~U • ~X   3 DeM.**
    5. **~(S v T)   4 DeM.**   5. **~~U   4 Simp.**
    6. **~~R   1,5 M.T.**   6. **U   5 D.N.**
    7. **R   6 D.N.**   7. **W   1,6 M.P.**

9. 1. A ⊃ (B • C)
    2. (B v C) ⊃ D / ∴ A ⊃ D
    3. ~A v (B • C)   1 Impl.
    4. (~A v B) • (~A v C) 4.
                          3 Dist.
    5. ~A v B   4 Simp.
    6. (~A v B) v C   5 Add.
    7. ~A v (B v C)   6 Assoc.
    8. A ⊃ (B v C)   7 Impl.
    9. A ⊃ D   8,2 H.S.

10. 1. E / ∴ F ⊃ F   (Hint: Use Impl. three
    2. E v ~F   1 Add.   times)
    3. ~F v E   2 Com.
    4. F ⊃ E   3 Impl.
    5. F ⊃ (F • E)   4 Abs.
    6. ~F v (F • E)   5 Impl.
    7. (~F v F) • (~F v E)
                         6 Dist.
    8. ~F v F   7 Simp.
    9. F ⊃ F   8 Impl.

11. 1. (G v H) ⊃ I
    2. (J v K) ⊃ ~I
    3. K / ∴ ~H
    4. K v J   3 Add.
    5. J v K   4 Com.
    6. ~I   2,5 M.P.
    7. ~(G v H)   1,6 M.T.
    8. ~G • ~H   7 DeM.
    9. ~H • ~G   8 Com.
    10. ~H   9 Simp.

12. 1. (L v M) ⊃ N
    2. P ⊃ M
    3. ~N / ∴ ~P • ~L
    4. ~(L v M)   1,3 M.T.
    5. ~L • ~M   4 DeM.
    6. ~M • ~L   5 Com.
    7. ~L   5 Simp.
    8. ~M   6 Simp.
    9. ~P   2,8 M.T.
    10. ~P v ~L   9,7 Conj.

Write out in English an argument (note: not the whole proof) that could be symbolized by the problems identified. Do they sound valid? Why or why not?

13. Problem #1   "I study logic. Therefore if it's snowing outside then I study logic." This doesn't really sound valid; the conclusion doesn't seem to be implied by the premise.

14. Problem #10   "I study logic. Therefore if it's snowing outside then it's snowing outside." This also doesn't seem valid. The premises and the conclusion are unrelated.

Exercise Twenty-five

Translate the following arguments into symbolic form. Write a formal proof of validity for each. Each proof requires no more than four additional steps.

1.   If evolutionary theory is correct then the biblical creation account is false. However, if the Bible is God's word then the biblical creation account is true. Therefore if evolutionary theory is correct then the Bible is not God's word. (E, C, G)

```
1. E ⊃ ~C
2. G ⊃ C   / ∴ E ⊃ ~G
3. ~C ⊃ ~G         2 Trans.
4. E ⊃ ~G          1,3 H.S.
```

2.   It is impossible to both spend eternity in heaven and be condemned hell. So if you go to heaven you will not be condemned to hell. (H, C)

```
1. ~(H • C)   / ∴ H ⊃ ~C
2. ~H v ~C         1 DeM.
3. H ⊃ ~C          2 Impl.
```

3.   If Jesus both helped others and argued rationally then he was not insane. If the gospel accounts are true then Jesus argued rationally and he helped others. Thus either the gospel accounts are false or Jesus was not insane. (H, A, I, G)

```
1. (H • A) ⊃ ~I
2. G ⊃ (A • H)   / ∴ ~G v ~I
3. G ⊃ (H • A)      2 Com.
4. G ⊃ ~I          3,1 H.S.
5. ~G v ~I         4 Impl.
```

4. If God and Satan are both omnipotent then our cosmology is essentially dualistic. God is omnipotent. We must conclude that if Satan is also omnipotent then our cosmology is dualistic. (G, S, D)

```
1. (G • S) ⊃ D
2. G      / ∴ S ⊃ D
3. G ⊃ (S ⊃ D)        1 Exp.
4. S ⊃ D              3,2 M.P.
```

5. If the heavens are infinite then I cannot comprehend them, but neither can I comprehend them if they come to an end. If the heavens are not infinite then they come to an end. In any case, I cannot comprehend the heavens. (I, C, E)

```
1. (I ⊃ C) • (E ⊃ C)
2. ~I ⊃ E      / ∴ C
3. ~~I v E            2 Impl.
4. I v E              3 D.N.
5. C v C              1,4 C.D.
6. C                  5 Taut.
```

6. Either Peter was a liar when he claimed that Jesus never lied, or Jesus never lied. If Peter was a liar when he made this claim then he was a hypocrite. Peter was no hypocrite. Therefore Jesus was no liar. (P, J, H)

```
1. P v J
2. P ⊃ H
3. ~H      / ∴ J
4. ~P                2,3 M.T.
5. J                 1,4 D.S.
```

Exercise Twenty-six

Write a formal proof of validity for the following arguments using the Conditional Proof.

1. 1. A ⊃ (B • C) /∴ A ⊃ B   2. 1. D ⊃ E /∴ D ⊃ (E v F)
    2. **A**   **C.P.A.**   2. **D**   **C.P.A.**
    3. **B • C**   **1,2 M.P.**   3. **E**   **1,2 M.P.**
    4. **B**   **3 Simp.**   4. **E v F**   **3 Add.**
    5. **A ⊃ B**   **2-4 C.P.**   5. **D ⊃ (E v F)**   **2-4 C.P.**

3. 1. G ⊃ H   4. 1. J ⊃ K
    2. G ⊃ I /∴ G ⊃ (H • I)   2. L ⊃ K /∴ (J v L) ⊃ K
    3. **G**   **C.P.A.**   3. **J v L**   **C.P.A.**
    4. **H**   **1,3 M.P.**   4. **(J ⊃ K) • (L ⊃ K)**
    5. **I**   **2,3 M.P.**   **1,2 Conj.**
    6. **H • I**   **4,5 Conj.**   5. **K v K**   **4,3 C.D.**
    7. **G ⊃ (H • I)**   6. **K**   **5 Taut.**
                       3-6 C.P.   7. **(J v L) ⊃ K**   **3-6 C.P.**

5. 1. M ⊃ N   6. 1. Q ⊃ (R • S)
    2. P ⊃ ~N /∴ ~M v ~P   2. (R v S) ⊃ T /∴ Q ⊃ T
    3. **M**   **C.P.A.**   3. **Q**   **C.P.A.**
    4. **N**   **1,3 M.P.**   4. **R • S**   **1,3 M.P.**
    5. **~~N**   **4 D.N.**   5. **R**   **4 Simp.**
    6. **~P**   **2,5 M.T.**   6. **R v S**   **5 Add.**
    7. **M ⊃ ~P**   **3-6 C.P.**   7. **T**   **2,6 M.P.**
    8. **~M v ~P**   **7 Impl.**   8. **Q ⊃ T**   **3-7 C.P.**

7. 1. U /∴ W ⊃ W   8. 1. X /∴ Y ⊃ X
    2. **W**   **C.P.A.**   2. **Y**   **C.P.A.**
    3. **W ⊃ W**   **2-2 C.P.**   3. **Y ⊃ X**   **2-1 C.P.**

9. 1.   (A ⊃ B) • (C ⊃ D)   / ∴ (A • C) ⊃ (B • D)
    2.   **A • C**   **C.P.A.**
    3.   **A**   **2 Simp.**
    4.   **A ⊃ B**   **1 Simp.**
    5.   **B**   **4,3 M.P.**
    6.   **C • A**   **2 Com.**
    7.   **C**   **6 Simp.**
    8.   **(C ⊃ D) • (A ⊃ B)**   **1 Com.**
    9.   **C ⊃ D**   **8 Simp.**
    10. **D**   **9,7 M.P.**
    11. **B • D**   **5,10 Conj.**
    12. **(A • C) ⊃ (B • D)**   **2-11 C.P.**

CHALLENGE: Solve problem nine without using the Conditional Proof.

Here is one way:
    1.   (A ⊃ B) • (C ⊃ D)   / ∴ (A • C) ⊃ (B • D)
    2.   (~A v B) • (~C v D)   1 Impl.
    3.   ~A v B   2 Simp.
    4.   (~C v D) • (~A v B)   2 Com.
    5.   ~C v D   4 Simp.
    6.   (~A v B) v ~C   3 Add.
    7.   (~C v D) v ~A   5 Add.
    8.   [(~A v B) v ~C] • [(~C v D) v ~A]   6,7 Conj.
    9.   [(B v ~A) v ~C] • [~A v (~C v D)]   8 Com.
    10. [B v (~A v ~C)] • [(~A v ~C) v D]   9 Assoc.
    11. [(~A v ~C) v B] • [(~A v ~C) v D]   10 Com.
    12. (~A v ~C) v (B • D)   11 Dist.
    13. ~(A • C) v (B • D)   12 DeM.
    14. (A • C) ⊃ (B • D)   13 Impl.

Exercise Twenty-seven

Write a formal proof of validity for the following arguments using Reductio ad Absurdum.

1.
1.	~P ⊃ (Q v R)	
2.	~Q	
3.	~R /∴ P	
4.	~P	R.A.A.
5.	Q v R	1,4 M.P.
6.	R	5,2 D.S.
7.	R • ~R	6,3 Conj.
8.	P	4-7 R.A.

2.
1.	(~P v Q) ⊃ (R • S)	
2.	~R /∴ P	
3.	~P	R.A.A.
4.	~P v Q	3 Add.
5.	R • S	1,4 M.P.
6.	R	5 Simp.
7.	R • ~R	6,2 Conj.
8.	P	3-7 R.A.

3.
1.	P ⊃ Q	
2.	Q v P /∴ Q	
3.	~Q	R.A.A.
4.	P	2,3 D.S.
5.	~P	1,3 M.T.
6.	P • ~P	4,5 Conj.
7.	Q	3-6 R.A.

4.
1.	P /∴ Q ⊃ Q	
2.	~(Q ⊃ Q)	R.A.A.
3.	~(~Q v Q)	2 Impl.
4.	~~Q • ~Q	3 DeM.
5.	Q • ~Q	4 D.N.
6.	Q ⊃ Q	2-5 R.A.

CHALLENGE: Solve problem three *without* using Reductio ad Absurdum.

1.	P ⊃ Q	
2.	Q v P / ∴ Q	
3.	Q	C.P.A.
4.	Q ⊃ Q	3-3 C.P.
5.	(Q ⊃ Q) • (P ⊃ Q)	4,1 Conj.
6.	Q v Q	5,2 C.D.
7.	Q	6 Taut.

Exercise Twenty-eight

This assignment should be done on a separate sheet of paper.

1. Write a formal proof of validity for the Destructive Dilemma. This can be done in two additional steps.

> 1. (P ⊃ Q) • (R ⊃ S)
> 2. ~Q v ~S / ∴ ~P v ~R
> 3. (~Q ⊃ ~P) • (~S ⊃ ~R)   1 Trans.
> 4. ~P v ~R   3,2 C.D.

2. Invent and name your own rule of inference. Then use that rule to solve a proof from a previous exercise in fewer steps than it was previously solved. Include both proofs for comparison.

> **Consequent Replacement Rule   (C.R.)**
> **p ⊃ (q • r)   /   ∴ p ⊃ (q v r)**

<u>Ex. 24, #9</u>

1. A ⊃ (B • C)		
2. (B v C) ⊃ D	/ ∴ A ⊃ D	
3. ~A v (B • C)	1 Impl.	
4. (~A v B) • (~A v C)		
	3 Dist.	
5. ~A v B	4 Simp.	
6. (~A v B) v C	5 Add.	
7. ~A v (B v C)	6 Assoc.	
8. A ⊃ (B v C)	7 Impl.	
9. A ⊃ D	8,2 H.S.	

1. A ⊃ (B • C)
2. (B v C) ⊃ D / ∴ A ⊃ D
3. A ⊃ (B v C) 1 C.R.
4. A ⊃ D   3,2 H.S.

3-7. Show the rules Modus Tollens, Absorption, Hypothetical Syllogism, Disjunctive Syllogism, and Addition to be unnecessary by writing formal proofs of validity for them without using those rules anywhere in your proofs. You may use any of the other rules of inference, the rules of replacement, the Conditional proof, and Reductio ad Absurdum.

3. Modus Tollens

1. P ⊃ Q
2. ~Q   / ∴ ~P
3. ~Q ⊃ ~P   1 Trans.
4. ~P   3,2 M.P.

4. Absorption

1. P ⊃ Q / ∴ P ⊃ (P • Q)
2. P   C.P.A.
3. Q   1,2 M.P.
4. P • Q   2,3 Conj.
5. P ⊃ (P • Q)   2-4 C.P.

5. Hypothetical Syllogism

1. P ⊃ Q
2. Q ⊃ R   / ∴ P ⊃ R
3. P   C.P.A.
4. Q   1,3 M.P.
5. R   2,4 M.P.
6. P ⊃ R   3-5 C.P.

6. Disjunctive Syllogism

1. P v Q
2. ~P   / ∴ Q
3. ~~P v Q   1 D.N.
4. ~P ⊃ Q   3 Impl.
5. Q   4,2 M.P.

7. Addition

1. P   / ∴ P v Q
2. ~(P v Q) R.A.A.
3. ~P • ~Q   2 DeM.
4. ~P   3 Simp.
5. P • ~P   1,4 Conj.
6. P v Q   2-5 R.A.

CHALLENGE: Show Constructive Dilemma to be unnecessary, thus reducing the necessary rules of inference down to only three.

Constructive Dilemma

```
 1. (P   Q) • (R   S)
 2. P v R    /  ∴ Q v S
 3. (~Q ⊃ ~P) • (~S ⊃ ~R)   1 Trans.
 4. ~Q ⊃ ~P                  3 Simp.
 5. (~S ⊃ ~R) • (~Q ⊃ ~P)   3 Com.
 6. ~S ⊃ ~R                  5 Simp.
 7. ~(Q v S)             R.A.A.
 8. ~Q • ~S                  7 DeM.
 9. ~Q                       8 Simp.
10. ~S • ~Q            8 Com.
11. ~S                      10 Simp.
12. ~P                      4,9 M.P.
13. ~R                      6,11 M.P.
14. ~P • ~R           12,13 Conj.
15. ~(P v R)                14 DeM.
16. (P v R) • ~(P v R)     2,15 Conj.
17. Q v S                  7-16 R.A.
```

Exercise Twenty-nine

Demonstrate that negation and conjunction together form a truth-functionally complete set. Use the numbers given to write your answers below.

1	2	3	4	5	6	7	8	9	10	11
T	T	T	T	T	T	T	T	F	F	F
T	T	T	T	F	F	F	F	T	T	T
T	T	F	F	T	T	F	F	T	T	F
T	F	T	F	F	F	F	T	T	F	T

12	13	14	15	16
F	F	F	F	F
T	F	F	F	F
F	T	T	F	F
F	T	F	T	F

1.   ~(p • ~p)   9.   ~(p • q)

2.   ~(~p • ~q)   10.   ~(p • q) • ~(~p • ~q)

3.   ~(~p • q)   11.   ~q

4.   p   12.   p • ~q

5.   ~(p • ~q)   13.   ~p

6.   q   14.   ~p • q

7.   ~(~p • q) • ~(p • ~q)   15.   ~p • ~q

8.   p • q   16.   p • ~p

CHALLENGE: Develop a conditional proposition p ⊃ q using only NOR.

$$[(p \; \triangledown \; p) \; \triangledown \; q] \; \triangledown \; [(p \; \triangledown \; p) \; \triangledown \; q]$$

TRUTH TREES

Exercise Thirty

Using the method of truth trees, determine the consistency of the following sets of propositions. Recover the truth values for all consistent sets.

1. { P, ~Q • R }

```
        1. P              S.M.
        2. ~Q • R √       S.M.
        3. ~Q             2•D
        4. R              2•D
               ○
```

consistent

P	Q	R
T	F	T

2. { ~ ~P, ~P • Q }

```
        1. ~~P √          S.M.
        2. ~P • Q √       S.M.
        3. P              1~~D
        4. ~P             2•D
        5. Q              2•D
             3×4
```

inconsistent

3. { P, ~Q, ~P v ~ ~Q }

```
        1. P                    S.M.
        2. ~Q                   S.M.
        3. ~P v ~~Q √           S.M.

        4. ~P        ~~Q √      3vD
           1×4         |
        5.             Q        4~~D
                      2×5
```

inconsistent

4. { ~P • Q, Q v R }

```
        1.   ~P • Q √       S.M.
        2.   Q v R √        S.M.
        3.      ~P          1•D
        4.       Q          1•D

        5. Q        R       2vD
           ○        ○
```

consistent

P	Q	R
F	T	T
F	T	F

Exercise Thirty-one

Using the method of truth trees, determine the consistency of the following sets of propositions. Recover the truth values for all consistent sets.

1. { A ⊃ B, A, ~B }

```
1.    A ⊃ B  √   S.M.
2.       A        S.M.
3.      ~B        S.M.
             /\
4.  ~A        B    1⊃D
    2×4      3×4
```

inconsistent

2.   { ~C, ~(C ⊃ D) }

```
1.      ~C          S.M.
2.  ~(C ⊃ D)  √     S.M.
3.       C         2~⊃D
4.      ~D         2~⊃D
       1×3
```

inconsistent

3. { E ⊃ ~F, ~E • F }

```
1.   E ⊃ ~F  √   S.M.
2.   ~E • F  √   S.M.
3.        ~E      2•D
4.         F      2•D
           /\
5.  ~E       ~F   1⊃D
        ○        4×5
```

consistent

E	F
F	T

4.   { G ≡ H, ~H, G }

```
1.  G ≡ H  √   S.M.
2.     ~H      S.M.
3.      G      S.M.
        /\
4.  G      ~G    1≡D
5.  H      ~H    1≡D
   2×5     3×4
```

inconsistent

5. { J ⊃ ~(J ≡ K), ~(J ⊃ K) }

```
    1.  J ⊃ ~(J ≡ K) √          S.M.
    2.     ~(J ⊃ K) √           S.M.
    3.         J                2~⊃D
    4.        ~K                2~⊃D           consistent

    5.  ~J      ~(J ≡ K) √      1⊃D            J    K
        3×5                                    ───────
    6.          J    ~J         5~≡D           T    F
    7.         ~K     K         5~≡D
                ○    3×6
```

6. { L ⊃ M, M ⊃ L, ~(L ≡ M) }

```
    1.              L ⊃ M √              S.M.
    2.              M ⊃ L √              S.M.
    3.            ~(L ≡ M) √             S.M.

    4.       L              ~L           3~≡D
    5.      ~M               M           3~≡D

    6.  ~L      M       ~L        M       1⊃D
        4×6    5×6
    7.              ~M   L   ~M    L      2⊃D
                   5×7 6×7  6×7  4×7
```

                                       inconsistent

Exercise Thirty-two

Using the method of truth trees, determine the consistency of the following sets of propositions. Recover the truth values for all consistent sets.

1. { A ⊃ B, (A • B) ⊃ C, ~(A • C), A }   (Hint: Each step need not have
                                                                            more than one branch)

```
     1.        A ⊃ B √                S.M.
     2.     (A • B) ⊃ C √             S.M.
     3.       ~(A • C) √              S.M.
     4.           A                   S.M.

     5. ~A              ~C            3~•D        inconsistent
        4×5

     6.        ~(A • B)      C        2⊃D
                             5×6

     7.    ~A          ~B             6~•D
           4×7

     8.         ~A          ~B        1⊃D
               4×8        7×8
```

2. { D ≡ (E ⊃ F), ~D • E, D ≡ F }

```
     1.      D ≡ (E ⊃ F) √      S.M.
     2.        ~D • E √              S.M.
     3.        D ≡ F √               S.M.
     4.          ~D                  2•D
     5.           E                  2•D

                                                    consistent
     6.   D            ~D            1≡D
     7. E ⊃ F      ~(E ⊃ F) √        1≡D         D    E    F
        4×6                                      ─────────────
                                                 F    T    F
     8.              E               7~⊃D
     9.             ~F               7~⊃D

    10.    D            ~D           3D
    11.    F            ~F           3D
          4×10          ○
```

3. { G ⊃ H, G v I, ~H, ~(I • ~G) }

```
1.              G ⊃ H √              S.M.
2.              G v I √              S.M.
3.               ~H                  S.M.
4.           ~(I • ~G) √        S.M.
                  /\
5.         ~G         H           1⊃D
                      3×5
             /\
6. G              I               2vD        inconsistent
   5×6          /\
7.      ~I         ~~G √           4~•D
        6×7
8.                  G             7~~D
                   5×8
```

4. { ~(J ≡ K), K ⊃ (~L v M), L • ~(K • M) }   (Hint: Give yourself plenty
                                                              of room)

```
1.                    ~(J ≡ K) √              S.M.
2.                 K ⊃ (~L v M) √             S.M.
3.                 L • ~(K • M) √             S.M.
4.                       L                    3•D
5.                   ~(K • M) √               3•D      consistent
                      /      \
6.            J               ~J           1~≡D    J   K   L   M
7.            ~K               K            1~≡D    ─────────────
              /\              /\                    T   F   T   T
8.      ~K   ~L v M √    ~K  ~L v M √       2⊃D     T   F   T   F
            /\   7×8         /\
9.        ~L   M           ~L   M           8vD
          4×9  /\          4×9  /\
10. ~K  ~M  ~K   ~M          ~K   ~M        5~•D
    ○   ○    ○  9×10       7×10  9×10
```

Exercise Thirty-three

FOR THIS EXERCISE YOU MAY OMIT LINE NUMBERS AND JUSTIFICATIONS

Decompose each of the following compound propositions to determine if it is a *self-contradiction*. Write YES if it is and NO if it is not.

1.   ~P • (P • Q)
          ~P
       P • Q
          P
          Q
          ×

                           YES

2.   P • ~ (P • Q)
                P
            ~ (P • Q)
               / \
           ~P   ~Q
           ×   ◯

                           NO

(P ⊃ P) ⊃ (Q • ~Q)
         / \
~ (P ⊃ P) √   Q • ~Q √
     P   Q
    ~P   ~Q
     ×   ×

                  YES

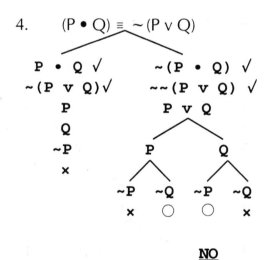

4.   (P • Q) ≡ ~ (P ∨ Q)

                           NO

Decompose the negation of each of the following compound propositions to
determine if it is a *tautology*. Write YES if it is and NO if it is not.

1. ~ [~ (P v Q) ⊃ ~ (P • Q)]   √
           ~ (P v Q)   √
           ~~ (P • Q)   √
                  P • Q   √
                     P
                     Q
                    ~P
                    ~Q
                     ×

                          YES

2.   ~ [~ (P • Q) ⊃ ~ (P v Q)]   √
               ~ (P • Q)   √
               ~~ (P v Q)   √
                      P v Q   √
                       P   Q
                   ~P   ~Q ~P   ~Q
                    ×   ○   ○   ×

                          NO

3. ~ [(P ⊃ Q) v (Q ⊃ P)]   √
           ~ (P ⊃ Q)   √
           ~ (Q ⊃ P)   √
                  P
                 ~Q
                  Q
                 ~P
                  ×

                          YES

4.   ~ [~ (P • ~Q) ≡ (Q v ~P)]   √

    ~ (P • ~Q) √   ~~ (P • ~Q) √
    ~ (Q v ~P) √   Q v ~P √
           ~Q   P • ~Q √
          ~~P √   P
             P   ~Q
        ~P   ~~Q √   Q   ~P
         ×   Q   ×   ×
                 ×

                          YES

Exercise Thirty-four

Decompose the negation of the biconditional of the two propositions to determine if they are equivalent. Write YES if they are and NO if they are not. Include line numbers and justifications, and recover the truth values which show non-equivalence.

1.

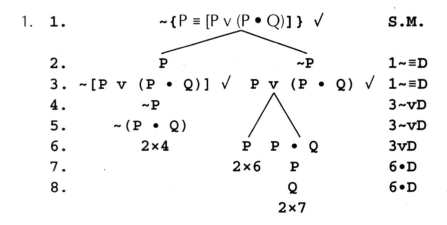

YES

2.

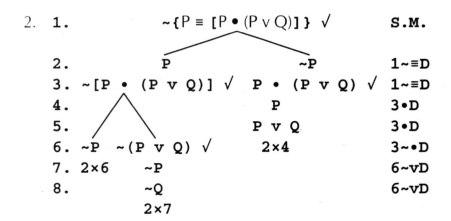

YES

3. 1.   ~[(P ⊃ Q) ≡ (Q ⊃ P)] √   S.M.

    2.   P ⊃ Q √   ~(P ⊃ Q)   1~≡D
    3.   ~(Q ⊃ P) √   Q ⊃ P   1~≡D
    4.   Q   3~⊃D
    5.   ~P   3~⊃D

    6. ~P   Q   2⊃D
        ○   ○

                                    NO   P   Q
                                                   ─── ───
                                                   F   T

4. 1. ~[(P ⊃ Q) ≡ (~Q ⊃ ~P)] √   S.M.

    2.   P ⊃ Q √   ~(P ⊃ Q) √   1~≡D
    3.   ~(~Q ⊃ ~P) √   ~Q ⊃ ~P √   1~≡D
    4.   P   2~⊃D
    5.   ~Q   2~⊃D

    6.   ~~Q √   ~P   3⊃D
    7.   Q   4×6   6~~D
    8.   ~Q   5×7   3⊃D
    9.   ~~P √   3~⊃D
    10.   P   9~~D

    11. ~P   Q   2⊃D
        10×11   8×11

                                    YES

Exercise Thirty-five

Use truth trees to determine the validity of the following arguments. If an argument is found to be invalid, recover at least one set of truth values which demonstrate the invalidity.

1.   A ⊃ B   B ⊃ C   ~C   ∴ ~A

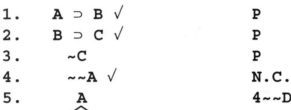

1.	A ⊃ B √	P
2.	B ⊃ C √	P
3.	~C	P
4.	~~A √	N.C.
5.	A	4~~D **VALID**
6. ~A B	1⊃D
5×6	
7. ~B C	2⊃D
6×7 3×7	

2.   D ⊃ E   F ⊃ E   ∴ D v F

1.	D ⊃ E √	P
2.	F ⊃ E √	P
3.	~(D v F) √	N.C.
4.	~D	3~vD
5.	~F	3~vD **INVALID**
6. ~D E	1⊃D
7. ~F E ~F E	2⊃D
○ ○ ○ ○	

D	E	F
F	T	F
F	F	F

3.   (G • H) ⊃ I   H   ∴ G ⊃ I

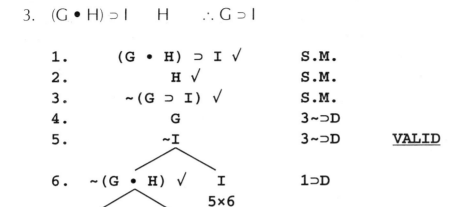

1.   (G • H) ⊃ I √   S.M.
2.   H √   S.M.
3.   ~(G ⊃ I) √   S.M.
4.   G   3~⊃D
5.   ~I   3~⊃D   **VALID**

6.   ~(G • H) √   I   1⊃D
                    5×6

7.   ~G   ~H   6~•D
    4×7   2×7

4.   If an axe was found in the safe then the butler put it there. If the butler put it there then he was guilty of the crime. If he was guilty of the crime then he would be distressed. He was not distressed. Either an axe was found in the safe or the safe was empty. Therefore the safe was empty. (A, B, C, D, E)

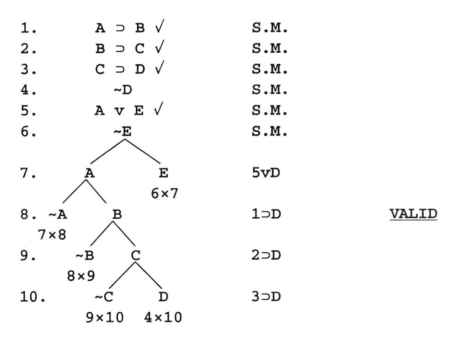

1.   A ⊃ B √   S.M.
2.   B ⊃ C √   S.M.
3.   C ⊃ D √   S.M.
4.   ~D   S.M.
5.   A v E √   S.M.
6.   ~E   S.M.

7.   A   E   5vD
                6×7

8. ~A   B   1⊃D   **VALID**
   7×8
9.   ~B   C   2⊃D
       8×9
10.   ~C   D   3⊃D
          9×10   4×10

5. If you studied logic then if you did not learn logic then you will not know how to do this problem. If you did not learn logic but you are brilliant then you will know how to do this problem. You know how to do this problem. Thus you either studied logic or you are brilliant (S, L, K, B).

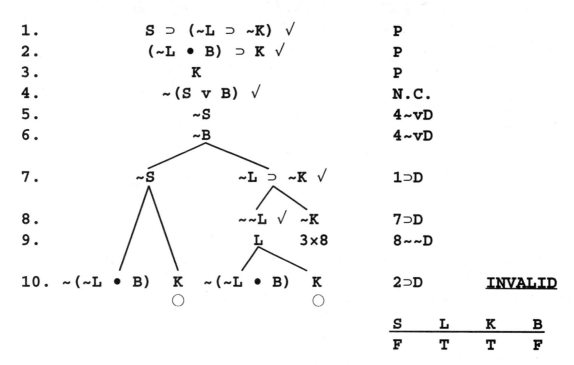

1.	S ⊃ (~L ⊃ ~K) √	P
2.	(~L • B) ⊃ K √	P
3.	K	P
4.	~(S v B) √	N.C.
5.	~S	4~vD
6.	~B	4~vD
7.	~S ~L ⊃ ~K √	1⊃D
8.	~~L √ ~K	7⊃D
9.	L 3×8	8~~D
10.	~(~L • B) K ~(~L • B) K	2⊃D **INVALID**

S	L	K	B
F	T	T	F